# RHYME TIME

# OXFORD
UNIVERSITY PRESS

Great Clarendon Street, Oxford OX2 6DP

Oxford University Press is a department of the University of Oxford.
It furthers the University's objective of excellence in research, scholarship,
and education by publishing worldwide in

Oxford   New York

Athens   Auckland   Bangkok   Bogotá   Buenos Aires
Cape Town   Chennai   Dar es Salaam   Delhi   Florence   Hong Kong
Istanbul   Karachi   Kolkata   Kuala Lumpur   Madrid   Melbourne
Mexico City   Mumbai   Nairobi   Paris   São Paulo   Shanghai
Singapore   Taipei   Tokyo   Toronto   Warsaw

with associated companies in   Berlin   Ibadan

Oxford is a registered trade mark of Oxford University Press
in the UK and in certain other countries

This selection and arrangement copyright © John Foster 2001

Illustrations copyright © Carol Thompson 2001

The moral rights of the author and artist have been asserted

First published 2001

British Library Cataloguing in Publication Data available

ISBN 0 19 276225 7 (hardback)
ISBN 0 19 276226 5 (paperback)

Typeset by Sarah Nicholson
Printed in Malaysia

RHYME TIME

# Around the Year

Compiled by JOHN FOSTER

Illustrated by CAROL THOMPSON

**OXFORD**
UNIVERSITY PRESS

# Acknowledgements

We are grateful to the authors for permission to include the following poems, all of which are published for the first time in this collection:

**Marie Brookes:** 'The Fair', and 'Holiday', both copyright © Marie Brookes 2001; **Sue Cowling:** 'First', copyright © Sue Cowling 2001; **Penny Dolan:** 'May Day', copyright Penny Dolan © 2001; **Eric Finney:** 'Mother's Day', copyright © Eric Finney 2001; **John Foster:** 'New Year Promises', 'Here is the Seed', 'Today's My Birthday', 'A Week at Gran's', and 'Advent Calendar', all copyright © John Foster 2001; **Jean Kenward:** 'Easter Egg' and 'Queen of the May', both copyright © Jean Kenward 2001; **Patricia Leighton:** 'Spring's Here' copyright © Patricia Leighton 2001; **Wes Magee:** 'Happy Eid' copyright © Wes Magee 2001; **Trevor Millum:** 'Summer Songs', copyright © Trevor Millum 2001; **Tony Mitton:** 'Snow Counting', 'Pancakes', 'Roundabout Rhyme', 'Carnival Time', 'Whizz, Crackle, Bang!', and 'Diwali', all copyright © Tony Mitton 2001; **Barbara Moore:** 'Chinese New Year' and 'Diwali', both copyright © Barbara Moore 2001; **Cynthia Rider:** 'A Harvest Prayer', copyright © Cynthia Rider 2001; **Andrea Shavick:** 'Hanukkah', copyright © Andrea Shavick 2001; **Erica Stewart:** 'Come to the Carnival', 'Happy New Year', 'Guru Nanak's Birthday', all copyright Erica Stewart 2001; **Charles Thomson:** 'A Present', copyright © Charles Thomson 2001; **Celia Warren:** 'What's Inside', copyright © Celia Warren 2001; **Brenda Williams:** 'The Easter Bunny' and 'The Train Journey', both copyright © Brenda Williams 2001.

We also acknowledge permission to include previously published poems:

**Moira Andrew:** 'November Night Countdown' first published in *Countdown* edited by Judith Nicholls (Ginn, 1999); 'Autumn Treasure' first published in *Racing the Wind* (Nelson, 1993) both reprinted by permission of the author; **Lucy Coats:** 'Off to the Sands' from *First Rhymes* (Orchard Books, a division of Watts Publishing Group Limited, 1994), copyright © Lucy Coats 1994, reprinted by permission of the publisher; **June Crebbin:** 'Goodnight' from *Cows Moo, Cars Toot* (Viking, 1995), copyright © June Crebbin 1995, reprinted by permission of Penguin Books Ltd; **Carolyn Graham:** 'Hallowe'en Parade' first published in *Holiday Jazz Chants* (OUP, 1999), reprinted by permission of the author; **Linda Hammond:** 'The Christmas Tree' and 'Sandcastle Fun' both from *Five Furry Teddy Bears* (Penguin, 1990), copyright © Linda Hammond 1990, reprinted by permission of the publisher; 'Roly Poly – Roly Snow' from *One Blue Boat* (Viking, 1991), copyright © Linda Hammond 1991, reprinted by permission of Penguin Books Ltd; **Shirley Hughes:** 'Spring Greens' from *Out and About* (Walker Books, 1988, 1998) copyright © Shirley Hughes 1988,1998, reprinted by permission of the publisher; **Wendy Larmont:** 'Chinese New Year' copyright © Wendy Larmont 1991, first published in *Special Days Poems – Catkins Poetry* (OUP, 1991), reprinted by permission of the author; **Marian Swinger:** 'Eid Mubarak', copyright © Marian Swinger 1992, reprinted by permission of the author; **Colin West:** 'The Farmer's Shadow' from *A Moment in Rhyme* (Hutchinson, 1987), copyright © Colin West 1987, reprinted by permission of the author.

Although we have tried to trace and contact copyright holders before publication, in one or two cases this has not been possible. If contacted we will be pleased to rectify the omission and any errors at the earliest opportunity.

# contents

## Autumn

## Winter

# Winter

# Happy New Year

It's midnight! It's midnight!
Hear the people cheer
As they wish each other
A Happy New Year.

It's midnight! It's midnight!
Hear the bells ring.
Wish for the things you'd like
The New Year to bring:

Health, wealth, and happiness
For you and me.
Health, wealth, and happiness
For all the family.

It's midnight! It's midnight!
Hear everyone cheer
As they wish each other
A Happy New Year.

*Erica Stewart*

# New Year Promises

This year I promise I'll be good.
I promise I'll do the things I should.

I'll pick my toys up off the floor.
I won't get cross and slam the door.

I won't get up early or stay up late.
I'll always shut the garden gate.

I'll eat my greens. I won't complain.
I'll never ever sulk again.

New Year promises are easy to make.
New Year promises are hard not to break.

*John Foster*

# Roly Poly — Roly Snow

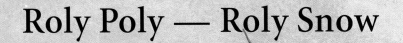

Roly poly, roly snow.
Roly poly, watch it grow.
First a big ball,
getting bigger.
Then a small ball
makes the figure,
of a snowman
round and fat,
with buttoned coat,
scarf, face, and hat!

*Linda Hammond*

# Snow Counting

One for a bobble hat, bright and red.

Two for the eyes on a snowman's head.

Three for the trees, so skinny and bare.

Four for the chimneys that smoke in the air.

Five for the footprints I've made in the snow.

Six for the flowerpots that hardly show.

Seven for the number of icicles I've found.

Eight for my snowballs, stacked on the ground.

Nine for my number of runs at the slide.

Ten for my footsteps to go back inside.

*Tony Mitton*

# Chinese New Year

Dragons, lions,
Red and gold.
In with the New Year,
Out with the old.

Banners flying,
Bands playing.
Lions prancing,
Dragon swaying.

Fireworks cracking,
Lanterns swinging,
People dancing,
Laughing, singing.

Dragons, lions,
Red and gold.
In with the New Year,
Out with the Old.

*Wendy Larmont*

# Chinese New Year

On the Chinese blossom tree,
Lucky bags for you and me!
Red and gold, what can they hide?
Let's find out, we'll look inside.
Silver coins, delicious sweets;
Lucky bags bring New Year treats!

*Barbara Moore*

# Happy Eid!

'Happy Eid!' we shout to all
as we run down the street.

We're on our way to Grandma's house
where friends and family meet.

We're all dressed in our very best
for this most special day.

At Gran's we'll give our gifts with love
and 'Happy Eid!' we'll say.

*Wes Magee*

14

# Eid-Mubarak

There's Granny, Uncle, Aunty,
my cousins at the back.
They're hugging Mum and Daddy.
We cry, 'Eid-Mubarak'.
We've had lots of cards
and presents,
there's a knocking at the door.
Can it be my grandad
bringing us some more?
Yes, it's really Grandad.
What's that behind his back?
We hug him in the hallway
and shout, 'Eid-Mubarak'.

*Marian Swinger*

# Pancakes

Pancakes, pancakes,
one by one.
Toss them, catch them,
just for fun.

Pancakes, pancakes,
two by two.
One for me
and one for you.

Pancakes, pancakes,
three by three.
Pancakes piled up
for my tea.

Pancakes, pancakes,
four by four.
Eat them up
and make some more.

Pancakes tossed up
in the air ...
Whoops! There's pancake
in my hair!

*Tony Mitton*

# Spring

# Spring's Here!

Tadpoles wiggle tails
Daffodils blow
Eggs hatch
Fledglings
Grow, grow, grow.

Sweet air, warm sun
Just a little rain
Blue sky
White clouds
Green leaves again.

Nights are getting lighter
More time to play
Spring's back
Three cheers!
Hip-hip-hurray!

*Patricia Leighton*

# Mother's Day

We really tried to spoil our mum
On Mother's Day:
Took her breakfast up to bed
On a tray;
Gave her presents, cards, and flowers —
A lovely bunch;
Did the washing up and cleaning,
Cooked the lunch.
Housework? We wouldn't let her
Lift a finger;
Put a CD on of Frank,
Her favourite singer.
We made the whole day for our mum
A real treat,
With lots of lovely things
To drink and eat.
Mum thanked us all and said,
'Today was bliss!
Could you please arrange for every day
To be like this?'

*Eric Finney*

# Spring Greens

Bulbs in pots,
Twigs in jars,
Dads in the street, washing cars.
Greens in season,
Trees in bud,
Sky in puddles,
Ripples in mud.
Birds in bushes, singing loud,
Sun tucked up in a bed of cloud.

*Shirley Hughes*

21

# Easter Egg

I like to paint
an Easter egg
in purple, green,
and blue,
and make a pattern
on the shell.
I might do one
for you.

And look! Here is
a funny egg
it wears a smiling
face,
with yellow spots
all over it!
I'll put it in
your place…

*Jean Kenward*

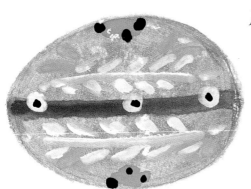

22

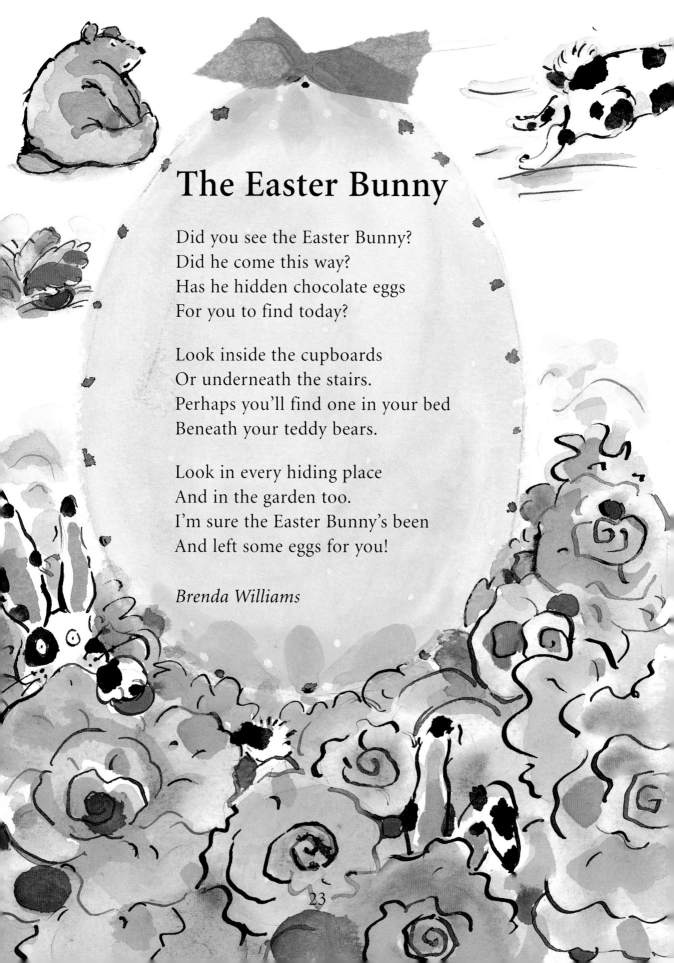

# The Easter Bunny

Did you see the Easter Bunny?
Did he come this way?
Has he hidden chocolate eggs
For you to find today?

Look inside the cupboards
Or underneath the stairs.
Perhaps you'll find one in your bed
Beneath your teddy bears.

Look in every hiding place
And in the garden too.
I'm sure the Easter Bunny's been
And left some eggs for you!

*Brenda Williams*

# Queen of the May

They say
yes, they say
that the Queen
of the May
is out to be
crowned
in the village
today!

The houses
are covered
with branches
of green
and specks
of white blossom
are twisted
between —

There's clapping
and skipping
and ribbons
and fun,
for the maypole
is up
and the dancing's
begun

And I heard
(yes, I heard
from a bird
in a tree)
that the Queen
of the May
may be someone
like ME.

*Jean Kenward*

# May Day

Around about the maypole
The rainbow ribbons dangle.

We went in and out as we were told —
So why are we in a tangle?

*Penny Dolan*

# I dig, dig, dig

I dig, dig, dig,
And I plant some seeds.
I rake, rake, rake,
And I pull some weeds.
I wait and I watch
And soon, you know,
My garden sprouts
And starts to grow.

*Anon.*

# Here is the Seed

Here is the seed,
Small and round,
Hidden underneath
The ground.

Here is the shoot,
Tiny and small,
Slowly, slowly
Growing tall.

Here is the sun
Here is the shower.
Here are the petals.
Here is the flower.

*John Foster*

27

# The Fair

Waltzers whizzing
round and round.
Crowds of people
on the ground.
Spinning wheels
and flashing lights
looking down,
from dizzy heights.

Win a goldfish.
Try your luck.
Knock down a coconut
Hook a duck.
Throw a hoop over a tin.
Pick your own prize
If you win!

Toffee apples
Fizzy drinks.
Cotton wool candyfloss
White and pink.
The smell of hot dogs
Fills the air.
Fun, noise, and music —
That's the fair.

*Marie Brookes*

# Roundabout Rhyme

I want to go on the firetruck
and ring its brassy bell.
I want to go on the speedboat
and the helicopter as well.

I want to go on the aeroplane
or maybe the motorbike.
It's hard to choose on the roundabout,
there are so many things I like.

*Tony Mitton*

# Today's My Birthday

Today's my birthday.
Now I'm four.
I'm one year older
Than I was before.

I measured myself
Against the wall
And I'm over a hundred
Centimetres tall —

Much taller than
I used to be,
When I was small
And only three.

Today's my birthday.
Now I'm four.
I'm older and bigger
Than I was before.

*John Foster*

100
50
40

# Summer

# Summer Song

Lying in the sunshine
Snoozing by the pool
Splashing in the water
Trying to keep cool

Wandering round the park
Doing this and that
That's what summer's all about
Being lazy as a cat

*Trevor Millum*

# Summer Song

Sing a song of summer
A pocket full of sand
Sing a song of summer
An ice cream in my hand

Sing a song of summer
A pocket full of shells
Sing a song of summer
And sniff the summer smells!

Sing a song of summer
A pocket full of rhymes
Sing a song of summer
I love the summer time!

*Trevor Millum*

# Holiday

Here is the car, and here are the cases.
Here are the children with happy faces.

Buckets and spades, balls and boats.
Food for a picnic, wellies and coats.

Here is the car with luggage piled high.
Here are the children waving Goodbye!

*Marie Brookes*

# A Week at Gran's

On Monday we went to the seaside
And I had a donkey-ride.

On Tuesday it rained all day.
We sat and played games inside.

On Wednesday we went to a fair
And I won a doll on a string.

On Thursday we went to the shops
Gran bought me this pretty ring.

On Friday we packed a picnic
And paddled in the pool in the park.

On Saturday we had a barbecue
And stayed up till it got dark.

On Sunday we packed our cases.
And Dad came in the afternoon.

As we waved goodbye, I shouted,
'Please can we come back soon!'

*John Foster*

# The Train Journey

The train is running on the

                                                track track track

And I'm sitting in the carriage at the

                                                back back back

For we're going on a journey that is

                                                fast fast fast

The fields and the cows whizz

                                                past past past

We're going to the seaside very

                                                quick quick quick

And I'm listening to the wheels as they

                                                click click click

And we're going over hills to the

                                                top top top

But slowly…
  very slowly…
    We come to a station and we

                                                stop…

                                                        *stop…*

                                                              *stop!*

*Brenda Williams*

36

# First

Can't wait to get there,
Pick up the key,
Drive to the chalet,
Can't wait to be
First to get changed
First to the pool,
First down the slide
Swish, splash — cool!

*Sue Cowling*

# Off to the Sand

Off to the sand,
Off to the sea,
Mummy and Daddy
And Teddy and me.

Sun's very hot,
Cream on my nose,
Dance in the waves,
Dabble my toes.

Buckets and spades,
Castles and moats,
Seagulls and seashells
And bobbing bright boats.

Ice-creams all melting
And lollies to lick,
Frisbees to throw
And beachballs to kick.

Wide open yawns
And eyelids that drop,
Pack up the picnic
For home's the next stop.

*Lucy Coats*

# Sandcastle Fun

I'm going to build a sandcastle
right here by the sea.
First of all it's very small
and then it grows like me.

I'll add some towers and windows,
give a final pat.
Then run, jump, and sit on it
and knock my castle flat!

*Linda Hammond*

# The Farmer's Shadow

Soft is the farmer's shadow
Upon the golden corn,
As we set off a-harvesting
In the early morn.

Swift is the farmer's shadow
When work is to be done
The straw we bundle into sheaves
In the midday sun.

Long is the farmer's shadow
As we all make our way
Along the path that takes us home
At the end of day.

*Colin West*

41

# Carnival Time

Sing me a song.
Tell me a rhyme.
Dance me a dance.
It's carnival time.

Put on a costume.
Paint your face.
Beat those drums
all over the place.

Sing me a song.
Tell me a rhyme.
Dance me a dance.
It's carnival time.

*Tony Mitton*

# Come to the Carnival

Come to the Carnival.
Hear the steelbands play.
Come to the Carnival.
It's Carnival Day today.

Dress up like a peacock.
Dress up like a king.
Dress up like a monkey.
Clap your hands and sing.

Dance like a princess
Tumble like a clown.
Stamp your feet to the beat,
Jump up and down.

Come to the Carnival.
Hear the steelbands play.
Come to the Carnival.
It's Carnival Day today.

*Erica Stewart*

# A Harvest Prayer

Thank You
for the food we eat.

For the bread that comes
from the shining wheat.

For the sweet black grapes
and honey from the bees.

For beans and yams
And fresh green peas.

For bananas and mangoes
and kiwi fruit.

For potatoes and rice
and red beetroot.

For apples and plums
and oranges sweet.

Thank You
for the food we eat.

*Cynthia Rider*

44

# Autumn

# A Fall of Colours

I like sunshine.
I like trees.
I like dancing
In the breeze.

I turn orange.
I turn brown.
I go sailing
To the ground.

I am crispy.
I can crunch.
I get raked up
In a bunch.

I get stuffed
In scarecrow sleeves.
My friends and I
Are AUTUMN LEAVES!

*Charles Ghigna*

# Autumn Treasure

Seeds on the wind,
travelling in the air,
seeds on parachutes
twirling everywhere.

Seeds from pepperpots
shaken on the ground,
seeds like catapults
shooting all around.

Seeds bright as jewels,
seeds on the wing,
seeds buried in the earth
ready for the spring.

*Moira Andrew*

# Hallowe'en Parade

Black cats, here they come!
Black cats, one by one.
Leaping, howling, having fun.
Black cats, here they come!

Skeletons dancing, here they come!
Skeletons dancing, one by one.
Shaking, rattling, having fun.
Skeletons dancing, here they come!

Witches flying, here they come!
Witches flying, one by one.
Witches on broomsticks, having fun.
Witches flying, here they come!

Spiders crawling, here they come!
Spiders crawling, one by one.
Creeping, crawling, having fun.
Spiders crawling, here they come!

*Carolyn Graham*

# Guru Nanak's Birthday

Today is very special.
It's full moon day, today.
We're going to the temple
To worship and to pray.

We'll listen to the stories
And share the festive food.
Everyone's excited
And in a happy mood.

Today is very special.
It's full moon day, today.
Today we're celebrating
Guru Nanak's Birthday.

*Erica Stewart*

# November Night Countdown

Ten fat sausages
    sizzling in the fire.
Nine fiery flames
    reaching ever higher.

Eight shining stars
    dropping on the ground.
Seven silver sparklers
    Whirling round and round.

Six golden fountains
    fizzing in the dark.
Five red rockets
    whizzing across the park.

Four bright Catherine wheels
    spinning on the gate.
Three wide-eyed children
    allowed out very late.

Two proud parents
    watching all the games.
One lonely Guy
    roasting in the flames.

*Moira Andrew*

# Whizz, Crackle, Bang!

Wait for the evening,
cool and dark.
Wait for the fizzle,
wait for the spark.

Whizz, crackle, bang!
Just watch us go,
golden rain
and sparkling snow.

Whizz, crackle, bang!
in the big, blue night,
making colours
for your delight.

Whizz, crackle, bang!
as we rush up high,
exploding colours
across the sky.

*Tony Mitton*

# Diwali

Light the candles, far and near,
Rama and Sita will soon be here!
Clean the house, bright as a pin,
And let the happy New Year in.
Diwali's here, let's dance and sing
For Rama, who will be the king.
The wicked demon's dead and gone,
Tell the news to everyone.
Light the candles, far and near,
Rama and Sita will soon be here!

*Barbara Moore*

# Goodnight

'Goodnight,' said the frog,
'I am burrowing deep
Into the mud for my winter sleep.'

'Goodnight,' said the hedgehog,
'I'm off to my nest,
It's time I went for a good long rest.'

'Goodnight,' said the bat,
'My feet are strong
I'll hang in a cave all winter long.'

'Goodnight,' said the dormouse,
'I shall be
Curled in my nest at the foot of the tree.'

'Goodnight,' said the toad,
'I've found a deep hole
To keep me warm from the winter's cold.'

'When you wake in the spring,'
Said the kindly sun,
'I'll be here with my warmth for everyone.'

*June Crebbin*

# Diwali

Fetch the candles.
Make it bright.
This is *our* festival
of light.

The goddess is coming
with luck and treats.
There's going to be laughter,
fireworks, and sweets.

Family and friends
are together tonight.
For this is Diwali,
our festival of light.

*Tony Mitton*

# Winter

# Hanukkah

Hanukkah, Hanukkah,
  Festival of light.
Candles burn, tops spin round,
  Time of great delight.
Hanukkah, Hanukkah,
  Let us dance and sing.
Candles burn, guests come,
What presents will they bring?

*Traditional*

# Hanukkah

Light the candles
Me and you
One, two

Pray for peace
Evermore
Three, four

Hold hands
Hug and kiss
Five, six

Always love
Never hate
Seven, eight.

*Andrea Shavick*

# Advent Calendar

Open the window.
What do you see?
A sprig of holly
A Christmas tree
Reindeer
Santa's sleigh
Mistletoe
A snowy day
A robin redbreast
A blazing fire
Christmas cards
A church choir
A box of crackers
A frozen pond
A Christmas cake
A fairy with a wand
A big parcel
A chocolate bar
A Christmas pudding
A toy car
An angel
A shining star
Shepherds on a hillside
A stable bare
Three wise men worshipping
The baby lying there.

*John Foster*

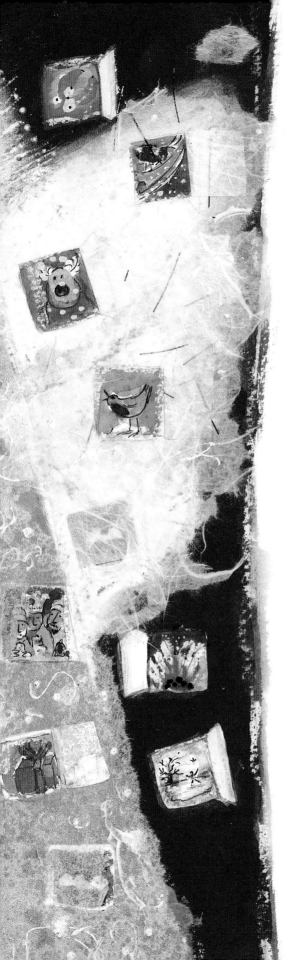

# The Christmas Tree

Dance with me, dance with me,
dance with me do.
Red streamers, green streamers,
then yellow and blue.
Dance with me, dance with me,
silver and white,
and help make our Christmas tree
pretty tonight.

*Linda Hammond*

# A Present

The cards are on the wall,
the lights are on the tree
and on the floor there is
a present that's for me.
It's red and green and blue
and big! … what can it be?

*Charles Thomson*

# What's Inside?

The round one rattles.
It feels like a kit.
The square one squeaks
if you press one bit.

The long one feels like
lots of sticks.
It might be a game
or a box of tricks.

My tummy feels like
a balloon about to burst!
Which new toy
shall I open first?

*Celia Warren*

# Index of Titles and First Lines
## *First lines are in italics*

# Index of Authors